S. Hrg. 113–460

THE FUTURE OF U.S.-CHINA RELATIONS

HEARING

BEFORE THE

COMMITTEE ON FOREIGN RELATIONS
UNITED STATES SENATE

ONE HUNDRED THIRTEENTH CONGRESS

SECOND SESSION

JUNE 25, 2014

Printed for the use of the Committee on Foreign Relations

Available via the World Wide Web: http://www.gpo.gov/fdsys/

U.S. GOVERNMENT PRINTING OFFICE

91–140 PDF   WASHINGTON : 2014

For sale by the Superintendent of Documents, U.S. Government Printing Office
Internet: bookstore.gpo.gov   Phone: toll free (866) 512–1800; DC area (202) 512–1800
Fax: (202) 512–2104   Mail: Stop IDCC, Washington, DC 20402–0001

(II)

CONTENTS

(III)

THE FUTURE OF U.S.–CHINA RELATIONS

WEDNESDAY, JUNE 25, 2014

U.S. SENATE,
COMMITTEE ON FOREIGN RELATIONS,
Washington, DC.

The committee met, pursuant to notice, at 2:15 p.m., in room SD–419, Dirksen Senate Office Building, Hon. Robert Menendez (chairman of the committee) presiding.

Present: Senators Menendez, Cardin, Corker, Risch, and Rubio.

OPENING STATEMENT OF HON. ROBERT MENENDEZ, U.S. SENATOR FROM NEW JERSEY

The CHAIRMAN. This hearing of the Senate Foreign Relations Committee will come to order.

We appreciate Ambassador Russel being with us, and our other panelists.

There is no question that one of our biggest foreign policy challenges is getting the relationship between the United States and China, and the rebalance to the Asia-Pacific, right. Today's hearing explores the U.S.-China relationship and, coming as it does just in advance of next month's U.S.-China Strategic and Economic Dialogue, allows us to reflect on other issues beyond the Middle East that will also shape the 21st century.

China is soon to become the world's largest economy, whether measured in purchasing price parity or raw GDP. Consider that more concrete has been poured in China in the past handful of years than in all of the United States during the 20th century. Eight of the world's 12-largest container ports are in China.

China is on the move, but the question is: On the move to what? Will China become a trade partner committed to the enforcement of international law, or will we see 19th-century mercantilist behavior and the flouting of international norms? Will China help to support peace and stability in Asia or seek to overturn the order? Will China open space for its citizens to express their views and ideas, or will it continue, like Cuba, to brutally repress its own people?

In the last year alone, a crackdown has swept away more than 150 journalists, lawyers, and activists. The bottom line is that there are reasons for hope, but there are also reasons for pessimism.

The fact is, U.S. exports to China have increased by almost $40 billion in the past 4 years alone, from $67 billion to $106 billion, creating and sustaining millions of U.S. jobs in sectors across the board: automobiles, power generation, machinery, aircraft, and other vital industrial sectors. That speaks to the potential of our partnership. At the same time, U.S. firms complain of cyber-enabled theft of intellectual property rights or just plain old-fashioned theft when trying to do business in China.

Equally or more troubling still, we have seen an increasingly provocative China on the seas, coercing and intimidating neighbors in both the East China Sea and South China Sea, and attempting to use the threat of military force to address territorial and regional disputes. China's provocative actions in the South China Sea threaten not just regional stability, but longstanding U.S. interests in the free flow of commerce, freedom of navigation, and in the peaceful diplomatic resolution of disputes consistent with international law. Likewise, China's continued deliberate and provocative actions in and around Japanese territory run the risk of sparking a broader regional crisis. There should be a clear cost to China's actions and what we must do to offset those actions is deepen our alliances with Korea, Japan, and the Philippines, and reconsider the arms embargo with Vietnam, and we must make sure we fully resource all elements of the rebalance.

So, I look forward to our panelists' thoughts on how we should evaluate the strategic and economic realities unfolding with the rise of China. How do we reconceptualize the problems we face? How do we turn them into opportunities? How do we make sure allies and partners have the resources they need in the context of China's rise? And how do we work with China through such mechanisms as the SSD at the Strategic and Economic Dialogue to assure that disagreements need not lead to conflict?

And, with that, let me recognize the distinguished ranking member, Senator Corker, for his remarks.

OPENING STATEMENT OF HON. BOB CORKER, U.S. SENATOR FROM TENNESSEE

Senator CORKER. Thank you, Mr. Chairman, and thank you for calling this hearing.

I also want to thank the witnesses for being here and sharing their wisdom with us.

It has been exactly 1 year since President Obama and President Xi Jinping gathered at Sunnylands to chart a new course for U.S.-China bilateral relations. Analysts were optimistic that the summit would set a tone for greater cooperation between the United States and China on a range of issues, including North Korea.

However, as we convene here, a year later, the prospects for enhanced cooperation seem fairly dim. Indeed, we are facing a period of increasingly strained relations between Washington and Beijing, with issues such as China's continued aggressiveness in the East and South China Seas, as well as serious ongoing issues with Chinese cyber theft.

Moreover, I am troubled that the Obama administration does not appear to have a clear China policy or a strategy to address Beijing's continued disregard for international norms, including economic rules of the road. It is deeply disconcerting to me that the negotiations on the Trans-Pacific Partnership, which has the potential to be a game changer in the Asia-Pacific by cementing free trade principles in the region and potentially influencing Chinese behavior, continue to drag on absent high-level political engagement from the administration.

The United States-China bilateral relationship is one of the most important and consequential relationships for U.S. political, economic, and strategic interests, yet China appears to be positioning itself increasingly as a geopolitical and strategic rival to the United States. The pace and lack of transparency with respect to the Chinese military modernization, coupled with China's actions in the East and South China Seas, has cast doubt on the idea of the peaceful rise of China.

Despite these challenges, I still see great opportunities to strengthen cooperation, specifically the conclusion of successful negotiations on Bilateral Investment Treaty, which has the potential to benefit U.S. businesses.

I look forward to hearing from Assistant Secretary Russel, and from our second panel of experts, on whether the time has come to rethink U.S. policy toward China and other issues I am sure they will bring up.

And again, I want to thank you, Mr. Chairman, for calling this hearing.

The CHAIRMAN. Thank you, Senator Corker.

Our first panelist is Daniel Russel, the Assistant Secretary of State for East Asia and Pacific Affairs.

Ambassador, your full statement is going to be included in the record, without objection. We would ask you to try to summarize it in about 5 minutes or so, so we can enter into a dialogue.

And, with that, you are recognized.

STATEMENT OF HON. DANIEL R. RUSSEL, ASSISTANT SECRETARY OF STATE FOR EAST ASIA AND PACIFIC AFFAIRS, U.S. DEPARTMENT OF STATE, WASHINGTON, DC

Ambassador RUSSEL. Thank you very much, Mr. Chairman, Ranking Member Corker. I appreciate the opportunity to testify today on United States-China relations. And I thank you also for your bipartisan support of our Asia policy.

I am also honored to participate with one of America's most accomplished diplomats, China experts, and a good friend of mine, Ambassador Roy, and with another important contributor, Dr. Friedberg.

This year marks the 35th anniversary of the official diplomatic relations between the United States and China. We have made remarkable progress during that time. There is enormous potential, moreover, for further progress that benefits both our countries, our neighbors, and the world.

To achieve this progress, we seek a relationship defined, not by strategic rivalry, but by fair and healthy competition, by practical cooperation on priority issues, and by constructive management of differences. As President Obama has made clear, we seek and welcome the emergence of a stable, peaceful, and prosperous China that respects and supports global rules and universal values. Our two economies are intertwined, so China's growth fuels our own and promotes the region's prosperity, a prosperity underpinned by America's enduring security commitments and engagement. Many of our interests coincide. So, China's expanding regional role can complement the sustained United States strategic engagement in the Asia-Pacific.

Mr. Chairman, we do not seek to contain China. To the contrary, we want China to contribute to the stability and development of the region by exercising restraint, by upholding the basic rules on which the international system is built, rules that China helps formulate and benefits from. So, to advance this goal, we maintain an intense pace of high-level bilateral engagement.

In 2 weeks, our countries will hold the U.S.-China Strategic and Economic Dialogue, the S&ED, in Beijing. This important annual dialogue is led by Secretaries Kerry and Lew, with their Chinese counterparts, and covers virtually every aspect of our relationship. The strategic track includes our highest ranking joint civilian-military exchange with China, will seek progress on challenges in Africa, South Asia, the Middle East, and will discuss concerns like maritime disputes and China's behavior in the South and East China Sea, as well as cyber security and terrorism, and will further our important efforts with China on the world's most pressing nuclear proliferation challenges: North Korea and Iran.

In the economic track, we will work to strengthen global economic recovery. China's leaders have announced plans for economic reforms that, if realized, could go a long way in moving China's economy toward fair market principles. Growing Chinese direct investment in the United States contributes to jobs here at home, and our Bilateral Investment Treaty negotiations hold the potential for greater benefit.

We will work on climate change, energy, and environment issues, where the United States and China share common interests and responsibilities as the two largest energy consumers and carbon emitters.

And we will raise our concerns about the worsening human rights situation, as senior U.S. officials invariably do. Just this month, for example, China harshly suppressed any commemoration of the 25th anniversary of the violent Tiananmen Square crackdown, with cases of harassment, detention, and arrests of journalists, lawyers, activists.

We will also expand exchange programs that foster long-term mutual understanding through the annual United States-China consultation on people-to-people exchanges—235,000 Chinese students studied in the United States last year, and we are increasing the number of Americans who study in China. And 1.8 million Chinese visitors last year contributed nearly $10 billion to our economy.

Mr. Chairman, the United States-China relationship has made great strides over these decades, and we are committed to building on that progress. Together, we seek to create a ''new model of relations'' built on practical cooperation and constructive management of differences that strengthens the international system to the benefit of our countries and the world.

Thank you, and I look forward to your questions.

[The prepared statement of Ambassador Russel follows:]

PREPARED STATEMENT OF DANIEL R. RUSSEL

INTRODUCTION

Chairman Menendez, Ranking Member Corker, members of the committee, thank you for the opportunity to testify today on U.S.-China relations. It is also a great honor to be participating in today's hearing with one of our Nation's most accomplished diplomats, Ambassador Stapleton Roy—a friend, former colleague, and one of the foremost experts on U.S.-China relations. Ambassador Roy's contributions to the U.S.-China relationship have been invaluable, and I look forward to hearing his insights.

I would also like to take this opportunity to thank you, Mr. Chairman, for your leadership and to acknowledge this committee's contributions to the rich bipartisan tradition of engaging China. I have found it extremely valuable to work closely with the committee's members, and in particular with the Asia Subcommittee, in advancing U.S. interests vis-a-vis China and the Asia-Pacific region as a whole.

OVERALL BILATERAL RELATIONS

This year marks the 35th anniversary of the establishment of official diplomatic relations between the United States and China. We have made remarkable progress since the era of back-channel messaging and secret trips. The scope of today's U.S.-China relationship was unimaginable when President Nixon made his historic visit in 1972 to China.

Yet there is still enormous potential for progress in the U.S.-China relationship. Progress that will yield benefits to the citizens of both countries, our neighbors, and the world. To realize this progress and these benefits, we seek to ensure that the relationship is not defined by strategic rivalry, but by fair and healthy competition, by practical cooperation on priority issues, and by constructive management of our differences and disagreements. Where interests overlap, we will seek to expand cooperation with China. These areas include economic prosperity, a denuclearized Korean Peninsula, peaceful resolution of the Iranian nuclear issue, and a reduction in the emission of greenhouse gases. Where they diverge—and we have significant and well-known areas of disagreement—we will work to ensure that our differences are constructively managed.

Mr. Chairman, there are those who argue that cold-war-like rivalry is inevitable and that the United States and China are condemned to a zero-sum struggle for supremacy, if not conflict. I reject such mechanistic thinking. As anyone who has served in government can tell you, this deterministic analysis overlooks the role of leaders who have the ability to set policy and to shape relationships. It gives short shrift to the fact that our two economies are becoming increasingly intertwined, which increases each side's stake in the success of the other. It undervalues the fact that leaders in Washington and Beijing are fully cognizant of the risk of unintended strategic rivalry between an emerging power and an established power and have agreed to take deliberate actions to prevent such an outcome. And it ignores the reality of the past 35 years—that, in spite of our differences, U.S.-China relations have steadily grown deeper and stronger—and in doing so, we have built a very resilient relationship.

We view China's economic growth as complementary to the region's prosperity, and China's expanded role in the region can be complementary to the sustained U.S. strategic engagement in the Asia-Pacific. We and our partners in the region want China's rise to contribute to the stability and continued development of the region. As President Obama and Secretary Kerry have made very clear, we do not seek to contain China; to the contrary, we welcome the emergence of a stable, peaceful, and prosperous China. We believe all countries, and particularly emerging powers like China, should recognize the self-benefit of upholding basic rules and norms on which the international system is built; these are rules and norms which China has participated in formulating and shaping, and they are rules and norms that it continues to benefit from. In this context, we are encouraging China to exercise restraint in dealing with its neighbors and show respect for universal values and international law both at home and abroad.

A key element of our approach to the Asia-Pacific region, often called the rebalance, is strengthening America's alliances and partnerships in the region. This contributes directly to the stable security environment that has underpinned the region's—and China's—dramatic economic growth and development.

A second element is working to build up regional institutions in order to uphold the international rules-based system and create platforms for the countries and leaders to work on priority strategic, economic, and other issues. These institutions help develop habits of cooperation and promote respect for the interests of all parties.

A third key element has been expanding and deepening our relationships with important emerging countries such as China, including through regular and high-level dialogue.

In just 2 weeks, our countries will hold the sixth round of the U.S.-China Strategic and Economic Dialogue—the ''S&ED''—in Beijing. This annual dialogue is unique in its level and scope. It is led on the U.S. side by Secretaries Kerry and Lew and brings a number of Cabinet-level and other senior U.S. Government officials together with their Chinese counterparts to work on the major issues facing us. The breadth of the agenda in the two tracks—strategic and economic—reflects the breadth of modern U.S.-China relations. The S&ED is an important vehicle for making progress in the pursuit of a cooperative and constructive relationship; for building a ''new model'' that disproves the thesis that the United States and China are somehow destined for strategic rivalry and confrontation.

The S&ED is an important forum for the United States and China to take stock of and set goals for the bilateral relationship, to review regional and international developments and explain our respective policies, to coordinate and seek practical areas of cooperation on important issues of mutual interest, and to constructively manage areas of difference through candid, high-level discussions.

Let me preview of some of the topics for upcoming discussions at this year's S&ED:

- We will exchange views and explore prospects for progress on regional challenges, including Sudan, Afghanistan, Iran, North Korea, Ukraine, Iraq, and maritime disputes in the South and East China Seas;
- The world's two largest economies will work on strengthening the global economic recovery;
- The world's two biggest energy consumers and carbon emitters will work on combating climate change, and expand cooperation on clean energy;
- We will discuss global challenges ranging from cyber security to counterterrorism to wildlife trafficking, and the United States will raise our concerns over human rights;
- Secretary Kerry will cochair the annual U.S.-China High-Level Consultation on People-to-People Exchange, which supports exchange programs that build the foundation for mutual understanding and trust;
- And Deputy Secretary of State Bill Burns and his Chinese counterpart will hold the U.S.-China Strategic Security Dialogue (SSD), our highest-ranking joint civilian-military exchange with China, where we will conduct frank discussions on some of the most sensitive strategic issues in the relationship.

The S&ED and our numerous other dialogues and official exchanges with the Chinese each year reflect the importance we attach to managing this relationship. This level and pace of engagement show the commitment of both sides to producing tangible benefits for our two peoples, the Asia-Pacific region, and the global community.

The United States and China have a vital stake in each other's success. That is why we maintain an intensive schedule of engagement; President Obama and President Xi met in Sunnylands, CA, a year ago and have met twice more since then. The President plans to visit Beijing in November when China hosts APEC. Secretary Kerry, as well as numerous Cabinet and sub-Cabinet officials, have visited China already in 2014 and have met with Chinese counterparts in the United States or at international fora.

We work with China in virtually all important international arenas, including the U.N., the G20, the East Asia Summit, and APEC where we are cooperating closely on regulatory transparency, supply chain efficiencies, promoting clean and renewable energy, cross-border education, and combating corruption and bribery. Our relationship touches on nearly every regional and global issue, and, as such, requires sustained, high-level attention. Moreover, few of these issues can be effectively addressed if China and the United States do not cooperate.

ECONOMIC RELATIONS

Economic issues play a central role in the U.S.-China relationship. China's economic success has added to our growth and increased the purchasing power of consumers in the United States. Our two-way trade has almost quadrupled since China joined the WTO in late 2001. While the long-standing imbalance in that trade remains troubling, China is now one of the fastest growing U.S. export markets. In fact, U.S. exports to China grew by more than 90 percent between 2007 and 2013. In our bilateral engagements, we are encouraging economic reforms within China to ensure not only that its economic behavior is sustainable on its own terms, but that it contributes to strong, sustainable and balanced growth of the global economy. This includes reorienting its economy away from a development model reliant on exports and credit-fueled investment in real estate and infrastructure to one that increases consumer spending and contributes to global demand. Central to this goal has been urging China to move toward a market-determined exchange rate. We are also addressing sources of friction in our bilateral relationship by pressing China to change a range of discriminatory policies and practices that harm U.S. companies and workers and that undermine incentives to innovate. These include subsidies that tilt the competitive playing field in favor of Chinese national champions, policies that pressure companies to hand over intellectual property as a condition for access to the Chinese market, and export credits that unfairly advantage Chinese companies in third markets. U.S. businesses have investments totaling over $50 billion. And from 2012 to 2013, Chinese direct investment flows into the United States more than doubled, according to private sector figures, and now contribute to thousands of jobs here. Our ongoing bilateral investment treaty negotiations hold the potential for even more mutually beneficial economic ties.

Even as we increase trade and investment, we will continue insisting on tangible progress in other economic areas that matter to the United States. These include:

- China continuing to move toward a market-determined exchange rate;
- Negotiating a Bilateral Investment Treaty;
- Increasing access to Chinese markets for U.S. businesses;
- Developing a more transparent regulatory regime;
- Ending industrial policies that favor state-owned enterprises and national champions and seek to disadvantage foreign companies and their products;
- Ending forced technology transfer; and
- Addressing U.S. concerns over the theft of intellectual property and trade secrets, including government-sponsored, cyber-enabled theft for the purpose of giving Chinese companies a competitive advantage.

We will also continue to encourage greater Chinese integration into the rules-based international economic and trading system, in order to create a level playing field for domestic and foreign companies operating in its and other markets. Over the last few months, China's leaders have announced plans for sweeping reforms that, if realized, could go a long way in moving China's economy toward market principles. We are encouraged that these announced reforms would potentially give the market a greater role in the economy, and we are keenly interested to see such reforms put into practice. I believe we can do much to work with China as it transitions to a consumption-driven, market-oriented growth model that would benefit both our economies.

MILITARY-TO-MILITARY RELATIONS

On the military side of the U.S.-China relationship, we are committed to building a sustained and substantive military-to-military relationship that focuses on identifying concrete, practical areas of cooperation and reducing risk. This includes not only deepening the use of institutionalized dialogue mechanisms, including senior defense participation at the SSD and S&ED, but also inviting the Chinese to join regional cooperative exercises and expanding talks with the Chinese military about operational safety in the region. For the first time this year, China will participate in RIMPAC June 26–August 1 in Hawaii.

We also aim to continue high-level exchanges between our militaries. Recent exchanges have included visits to China by Secretary Hagel in April and General Odierno in February, and a visit to the United States by Chief of the General Staff, General Fang Fenghui, in May.

At the same time, we will continue to carefully monitor China's military developments and encourage China to exhibit greater transparency with respect to its military spending and modernization. This will help countries better understand the motivations of the People's Liberation Army. We continue to encourage China to use its military capabilities in a manner conducive to the maintenance of peace and stability in the Asia-Pacific region.

GLOBAL AND REGIONAL ISSUES

As the largest energy consumers, greenhouse gas emitters, and renewable energy producers, the United States and China share common interests, challenges, and responsibilities. These are issues that relate directly to our economic and national security. Cooperation on climate change, energy, and environmental protection is more critical than ever and is an important area of focus in the U.S.-China bilateral relationship.

Through broad dialogues such as the Ten-Year Framework for Energy and Environment Cooperation and the S&ED, over the last year we have been able to produce new and expanded commitments to cooperation on climate change, energy, and the environment. During Secretary Kerry's February trip to Beijing, he announced implementation plans for each of the five initiatives under the Climate Change Working Group as well as a new enhanced policy dialogue on domestic and international policies to address climate change that will be held on the margins of the upcoming S&ED.

China is a vital partner on some of the world's most pressing proliferation challenges, including the DPRK and Iran. The United States and China agree on the importance and urgency of achieving a denuclearized, stable, and prosperous Korean Peninsula. While differences remain between us on some of the tactics, we coordinate closely and consult intensively on how to advance these shared goals. The result has been a tightened web of sanctions targeting North Korea's nuclear, ballistic missile, and proliferation efforts. China has also strengthened its own sanctions enforcement, which we welcome, though it could do more to prevent North Korea from engaging in proliferation activities. Indeed, North Korea remains in flagrant violation of the U.N. Security Council resolutions that the United States and China approved and support. So we are urging China to make greater use of its unique leverage with the DPRK to produce concrete signs that the DPRK leader has come to the realization that his only viable path forward is denuclearization.

On Iran, the United States and China share the goal of preventing Iran from acquiring a nuclear weapon and are working together within the P5+1 negotiations with Iran toward that goal. Through our frequent and high-level engagement, we will continue to press China to honor its commitments, in particular those related to its imports of Iranian oil and enforcement of U.N. sanctions, in furtherance of reaching a comprehensive and long-term solution to the Iran nuclear issue.

MANAGING DIFFERENCES

In the Asia-Pacific region, Beijing's neighbors are understandably alarmed by China's increasingly coercive efforts to assert and enforce its claims in the South China and East China Seas. A pattern of unilateral Chinese actions in sensitive and disputed areas is raising tensions and damaging China's international standing. Moreover, some of China's actions are directed at U.S. treaty allies. The United States has important interests at stake in these seas: freedom of navigation and overflight, unimpeded lawful commerce, respect for international law, and the peaceful management of disputes. We apply the same principles to the behavior of all claimants involved, not only to China. China—as a strong and rising power—should hold itself to a high standard of behavior; to willfully disregard diplomatic and other peaceful ways of dealing with disagreements and disputes in favor of economic or physical coercion is destabilizing and dangerous.

The United States does not take sides on the sovereignty questions underlying the territorial disputes in the South and East China Seas, but we have an interest in the behavior of states in their management or resolution of these disputes. We want countries, including China, to manage or settle claims through peaceful, diplomatic means. For example, the Philippines and Indonesia have just done so in connection with their EEZ boundary. Disputes can also be addressed through third-party dispute resolution processes. Where parties' rights under treaties may be affected, some treaties provide for third-party dispute settlement, as is the case of the Law of the Sea Convention, an avenue pursued by the Philippines in an arbitration with China currently being considered by an Arbitral Tribunal constituted under that treaty. The United States and the international community oppose the use or the threat of force to try to advance a claim, and view such actions as having no effect in strengthening the legitimacy of China's claims. These issues should be decided on the basis of the merits of China's and other claimants' legal claims and adherence to international law and norms, not the strength of their militaries and law enforcement ships or the size of their economies.

Another area where we believe China's actions run counter to important universal principles is the worsening human rights situation in China. Just this month, China conducted a harsh crackdown on commemorations of the 25th anniversary of Tiananmen Square. China's actions included the detention, harassment and arrests of journalists, lawyers, and activists. Top U.S. officials raise our concerns with Chinese leaders on a regular basis, and, as we have in every previous round, Secretary Kerry plans to raise human rights at this year's S&ED. We express concern about the Chinese Government's censorship of the media and Internet. We push for the release of all political prisoners, including but not limited to prominent figures like Liu Xiaobo. We urge China to address the policies in Tibetan areas that threaten the distinct religious, cultural, and linguistic identity of the Tibetan people. Instability and violence are on the increase in the Xinjiang Uighur Autonomous Region. As we unequivocally condemn the acts of terrorism and violence, we also urge China to take steps to reduce tensions and reform counterproductive policies that stoke discontent and restrict peaceful expression and religious freedom.

CONCLUSION

Clearly, a wide-ranging and complex relationship such as ours with China comes with challenges. Some degree of friction is inevitable. But an essential tool for managing and resolving differences is open and extensive communications between our two countries—at senior and working levels of government, military to military, through local governments and organizations, between our business communities, and at the grassroots level.

We are now reflecting on the considerable progress attained in 35 years of bilateral relations. One key lesson is that to ensure that our relationship grows and matures, we need to build up the links among our two peoples. People-to-people exchanges are essential to enhancing mutual understanding and furthering U.S. strategic and economic goals. To that end, the United States in 2013 received 1.8 million Chinese visitors who collectively spent $9.8 billion on goods and services in our economy. Our State Department personnel work hard to facilitate growing Chinese demand for international travel by maintaining average visa wait-times under 5 days over the past 2 years.

Education also plays an important role fostering mutual understanding. In 2013, we had 235,000 students from China studying in the United States, more than from any other country, and the United States aspires to increase the number of American students studying in China and learning Mandarin through the 100,000 Strong Initiative. In March, PRC First Lady Peng Liyuan welcomed First Lady Michelle Obama to China where together they met with U.S. and Chinese students and faculty and promoted the value of study abroad and educational exchange.

We are also working with groups like the Sister Cities International and the U.S.-China Governors Forum. These programs help by encouraging and supporting cities and states to deepen their cultural or commercial ties with Chinese counterparts. In the last year alone, we have supported numerous visits of governors and state delegations and helped them to find opportunities to deepen their involvement and links to China.

The Department works closely with the United States Chamber of Commerce, AmCham China, the U.S.-China Business Council, and other business groups to support key priorities for U.S. companies doing business in China and to promote greater Chinese investment in the United States. In partnership and consultation with those organizations, we have encouraged the Chinese Government to eliminate investment restrictions, strengthen IPR protection, increase regulatory transparency, and establish a level playing field for all companies in China.

In conclusion, let me paraphrase what President Obama said earlier this year when he met with Chinese President Xi at the Nuclear Security Summit in The Hague. The U.S.-China relationship has made great strides over these past several decades, and both sides are committed to building a new model of relations between our countries defined by expanded cooperation and constructive management of differences.

Mr. Chairman, I thank you for the opportunity to appear before you today to discuss U.S.-China relations. I look forward to answering any questions you and others from the committee may have.

The CHAIRMAN. Well, thank you. It sounds like a rather rosy picture. Let me delve into it a little bit.

So, when China speaks of a new type of great power relationship, what is it that the administration interprets in that phrase? Is that China just laying down a marker for gaining greater say in its own backyard? And what is our response to that?

Ambassador RUSSEL. The new model concept is something that was discussed indepth in the Sunnylands meeting, a year ago, that Senator Corker referred to. There are those in China who seek to define a new model as if it were the creation of a sphere of influence by China in the Asia-Pacific region, and the ''respect'' by the United States and the international community for certain ''core interests,'' as if it was not legitimate for the United States and others to hold positions on certain issues.

We see the prospect of a so-called ''new model'' very differently. To the President and to the administration, to the United States, the goal is a model that is defined by practical cooperation on issues of genuine significance to the United States, China, and to the world—real issues, not boutique issues—along with the ability and the wherewithal to address and manage our serious and genuine differences, and to do so in a way that is strengthening, not deleterious, to the rules of the international system that have allowed China to achieve so much progress in its development. We seek a model of a relationship that is marked not by strategic rivalry, but by healthy competition.

The CHAIRMAN. So—and that is what we see. What does China see when it says that it seeks a relationship that is based on a new great power paradigm?

Ambassador RUSSEL. When the Chinese officials talk about the ''new model,'' typically they talk about win-win outcomes, and they talk about respect for core interests. We are all for win-win outcomes, but we are not for slogans.

What we care about and what we seek to achieve is meaningful cooperation. So, at the upcoming S&ED, for example, on the security—on the strategic track, which, as I mentioned, brings together high-level civilian as well as military officers in the strategic security dialogue under it, we engage on issues like the conduct of China in the South China Sea and the East China Sea. We engage directly on issues of human rights, including the repressive practices in Xinjiang and Tibet. We do not consider so-called ''core interests'' to be out of bounds for substantive discussion, and we hold China to account for its behavior.

The CHAIRMAN. Well, when we talk about hoping that China will be part of an international order that will observe international rules, and you talk about the South China Sea, is our carefully calibrated balance between cooperation and competition still the right approach? Should we be putting a little more on the competition side and demonstrating, in more robust terms, our enduring national interest in freedom of navigation, the free flow of commerce, and the peaceful resolution of disputes, consistent with international law?

Ambassador RUSSEL. Mr. Chairman, we believe that competition and cooperation coexist in the United States-China relationship. We seek healthy competition on the basis of a set of accepted global norms. We welcome the right and the ability of China to participate in shaping and updating rules, but on the condition that China accepts that rules are binding on it, as well as on others. Rules apply not only to small countries, but to large ones.

We are strengthening our diplomatic engagement throughout the region. We have significantly strengthened our military alliances and our security relationships. Our presence in the life and in the security of the Asia-Pacific is robust.

The Prime Minister of Singapore is in Washington today. I think he had the opportunity to call on you and other members of the committee. Singapore, for example, is not only an important security partner of the United States, not only an important conegotiator in the effort to achieve a uniquely high-standard, comprehensive trade agreement, the TPP. Singapore is also a charter member in ASEAN, a regional grouping that the Obama administration has invested a great deal of diplomatic effort in supporting.

The CHAIRMAN. I appreciate that. But, you know, this committee has expressed itself, as has the Senate, about its concerns about the way China is acting in the South China Sea. And, while there may be—maybe those are legitimate disputes on territories—but the manner in which, so far, it seems to be addressed is more of a muscular China versus a China driven by the international order which seeks to solve its disputes through the international order. And that is a concern.

Let me turn to another concern. We talk about competition. I was in China last August, and throughout the region, and I always try to meet with the American Chamber of Commerce in different countries to get a perspective of the realities on the ground about the challenges of doing business for American companies in a given country. And a 2013 American Chamber of Commerce China survey found that 72 percent of respondents, which reflected a lot of what I heard when I was there, said that China's IPR enforcement was either ineffective or totally ineffective. The U.S. International Trade Commission estimated that United States intellectual-property-intensive firms that conducted business in China lost $48 billion in sales, royalties, and license fees in 2009 because of IPR violations there. In certain sectors, such as wind power, where American Superconductor has been severely harmed by IP theft by its Chinese partner, Sinovel, the damage to U.S. businesses have been particularly acute. It is estimated that an effective IPR enforcement regime in China that would be comparable to United States levels could increase employment by IP-intensive firms here in the United States by 923,000 jobs.

So, where does intellectual property rights in our competition and discussion with China rank on the list of priorities among the wide range of issues that we have with China?

Ambassador RUSSEL. Mr. Chairman, the protection of intellectual property rights is a top priority for the administration, and I can personally attest to the fact that President Obama, Vice President Biden, Secretary Kerry, and other Cabinet Secretaries have raised our concerns very directly with Chinese leaders, including, and particularly, the Premier, Li Keqiang, who has responsibility for the economy. This is on the agenda as a priority issue for the upcoming S&ED.

The CHAIRMAN. But, we have had this on the agenda. Now, this is not new to the agenda, right? So, what——

Ambassador RUSSEL. Right.

The CHAIRMAN [continuing]. Is the progress we have made? I mean, where has the dialogue taken us on making advancements? So far, I do not see it.

Ambassador RUSSEL. Well, there are points of measurable progress with respect to motion pictures, with respect to pharmaceuticals. But, I fully agree with your point that China still has a long way to go to meet acceptable international standards in protecting IPR.

One thing that is different is the fact that the Chinese themselves now realize that they increasingly have more to lose as Chinese companies develop products and as Chinese consumers suffer from the poison or the other deleterious effects of fake pharmaceuticals and counterfeit products.

We use our regular working group on IPR to delve down on very specific issues. We have made a strong push to educate Chinese consumers and manufacturers to the fact that they lose in the race for innovation, they lose in the race for entrepreneurship, when they flagrantly violate the rule of law and they rely on the theft or the forced transfer of U.S. or other technology and products as the driver of their industries.

A related problem, Mr. Chairman, is the use of cyber-enabled theft of United States companies' intellectual property and proprietary information, theft that we have identified as enabled, in some cases, by Chinese Government or Chinese military officials. This is an issue that we raise forcefully, and it is an area where we will continue to push for Chinese to take action.

The CHAIRMAN. I have many other questions.

Let me turn to Senator Corker, recognizing that there is a vote that is ongoing.

Senator Cardin, have you voted in the last vote?

Senator CARDIN. I have.

The CHAIRMAN. So, I will let Senator Cardin chair. I will leave, come back, and we will try to keep the hearing going, in respect to everybody's time.

Senator Corker.

Senator CORKER. Thank you. Thank you.

Again, thank you for being here.

I cannot help but notice that Secretary Kerry's bigger issues, timewise, seem to lie in the Middle East. Secretary Sherman is spending 100 percent of her time on Iran negotiations—we had a good meeting this morning—and Secretary Burns is leaving. Who is responsible at the State Department for our China policy?

Ambassador RUSSEL. Secretary Kerry, personally, is responsible, and is engaged directly in overseeing our China policy. I met with Secretary Kerry at some length last week to discuss it. I have accompanied Secretary Kerry to China. I will again next week, when he makes his sixth visit to Asia. He is on the phone with his Chinese counterparts, he is in regular receipt of the reports that our Ambassador, Ambassador Baucus, submit or that I send up. I have found, and I can attest, Senator, to the fact, that Secretary Kerry and Deputy Secretary Burns and all of our Under Secretaries are focused and engaged on the Asia-Pacific broadly, but particularly on the United States-China relationship.

Senator CORKER. And what is their constructive policy to persuade China to not have the antagonistic relations that it has with its neighbors?

Ambassador RUSSEL. Well, we have outlined clearly the principles that we believe should guide China and all the countries in the region with respect to maritime security, which includes, obviously, the respect for freedom of navigation and overflight, unimpeded lawful commerce, and insist that only peaceful resolution of disputes is in consistency with international law as the acceptable vehicle for responding.

There is, however, as you have pointed out, Senator, a pattern of behavior on the part of the Chinese that is straining China's relations with its neighbors and raising questions about China's intention. We talk candidly, directly, and openly to the Chinese leadership through our diplomatic context. We talk extensively with not only the other four claimants, which are ASEAN countries, but also the relevant neighbors who have a stake in the peaceful and open region in Southeast Asia.

We have put forward—and you will hear more about this from Secretary Kerry—a proposal that the claimants themselves, including China—China is not alone in overreaching—can, on a voluntary basis, forgo some of the provocative actions that are destabilizing, such as the reclamation of islands and the construction of bases, such as the building up of outposts, and so on.

So, we use public messaging, we use diplomacy. We also engage in building the capacity of the countries in Southeast Asia to ensure that they are able to adequately police their own territorial waters and that they can maintain the domain awareness that ensures that they know what is going on in their contiguous waters or in the open seas.

Our strategy, Senator, includes the support for a unified and influential ASEAN, and we believe that the call from the ASEAN countries to China to work with them, not to bully them, has a long-term salutary effect.

Lastly, the fact of the matter is that the robust military presence, the strong security commitments, and the healthy alliances that the United States maintains with many countries in the region similarly serves to maintain stability and keep the peace, going forward, as it has for the last six decades.

Senator CORKER. I appreciate that comprehensive answer. We just had a gentleman in from the region who is very much a part of China, if you will, and I asked him why this was taking place. If you want to synthesize his answer down to just a phrase, it was, ''China's doing this because they can.''

Ambassador RUSSEL. That is——

Senator CORKER. So, for years, they could not. They were not strong enough. Now they are a rising nation, and they can do what they are doing because they can.

I listen to you, and, I am not in any way trying to be critical of you as an individual, but I hear all those things, and it does not appear to me that it is having the desired outcome. Now, maybe over the next 20 years, as you build these capacities, maybe that is the case. But, I am concerned that, over the next 20 months, something happens that ends up creating a conflict or things get out of hand. I am just wondering what are some of the other things the administration might consider to ensure that something really catastrophic does not occur?

Ambassador RUSSEL. Well, thank you, Senator.

We believe strongly that diplomacy is the right vehicle for addressing this set of problems. We also think that one critically important step will be for all of the claimants, not only China, but particularly China, to define its claims clearly in ways that are consistent with international law. Because the risk of an incident and confrontation that you allude to is driven by ambiguity over who is claiming what, and on what basis. And so, we have, therefore, urged China to set aside the legally ambiguous construct of a nine-dash line and, instead, make its claim—and we do not take a position; its claims may be valid—but, make a claim in terms that are consistent with international law.

Number two, to pursue diplomatic or legal means to address it. We are also, as I mentioned, strengthening the capacity of the partners on an ongoing basis. I do not think this is a 20-year proposition, but it is not an overnight proposition, either.

China's—by its own assertion, China's interests lie in a stable and peaceful periphery. China has said—China's leaders have said that they want quiet in their environment in order to concentrate on development and social and economic growth. They have not achieved stability or quiet. To the contrary, they have generated real strains in their relationships. And so, the watchword that we advocate, in the first instance, is restraint, and big countries have a big responsibility to exercise it. Secondly, there are a range of very practical crisis-prevention and crisis-management initiatives that are in play in the region. And Secretary Kerry, who will be in the region for a seventh time to attend the ASEAN Regional Forum in August, is a strong advocate for, and has held in-depth discussions, as he will again in August, on some of these very practical confidence-building measures and crisis-prevention measures that include hotlines and that include agreements on handling unplanned incidents at sea.

Senator CORKER. Well, thank you for being here.

I am going to turn it over to Chairman Cardin and go vote so folks back home will have confidence in me. Okay? [Laughter.]

Thank you.

Senator CARDIN [presiding]. Secretary Russel, let me thank you for not just your leadership on the bilateral relations between the United States and China, but your work in East Asia and the Pacific and the manner in which you have worked with this committee and with the United States Senate. I do appreciate the close relationship and the sharing of information as we do the rebalance to Asia. I think it is been in the best interests of the United States.

And, as you point out, the bilateral relationship between the United States and China is multifaceted. There are areas where we have common interests, and we can, hopefully, find a path forward. One of those, quite frankly, is a peaceful resolution of the conflicts within the China Sea. It is not in China's interest to see military flareups or have this become expanded, because they depend upon commerce on the China Sea, as we do, as the region does. So, in my conversations with Chinese leaders, I think that they truly do not want to see a military flareup on the China Seas, and they want to keep the lanes open. But, it will take real leadership to have the rule of law prevail rather than the force of one country in determining the territorial disputes.

We have a common interest on the environment. And it seems to me we can work together on that. We have some common interests in trade. The United States market is very important to China, and commerce between China and the United States is very important to America's economy. So, we have a lot of common interests. And, as you point out, we have some significant challenges.

The Chinese progress on basic human rights is still very troublesome. The ability to express views contrary to the government in a safe and peaceful manner is certainly very much in question. The freedom of religion is a major issue and the protection of intellectual property. It is clear there are a lot of issues that need to be managed between the United States and China.

I found one thing you said about U.S. intentions which I could not agree with you more on. Our intention is for China to continue to grow and be a constructive player in the region. We are fully prepared to compete with any country in the world, including China, as long as it is on a level playing field. But we also need markets for our products. And as China's middle class grows, it provides consumers to buy American goods. So, our intentions are clearly for China to continue its economic growth, and do it in a way consistent with the respect for its neighbors, and to be a constructive player in the region.

But, I must tell you, in my conversations with Chinese leaders, I do not think they believe that. Seems to me they believe that we are interested in holding China back and that the rebalance is more about keeping China isolated than it is about every country in the region growing.

So, can you just share with us your view, if you agree with me—if you disagree with me, please let me know—as to how we deal with creating better trust between the United States and China, and do it in a way that does not compromise our positions on issues and our values, that we are pretty clear about what we expect in that relationship.

Ambassador RUSSEL. Well, Senator Cardin, first of all, thanks for your kind words, and thank you particularly for your leadership, especially on the Asia Subcommittee.

I very much agree with the points that you made in your statement. And I am very focused on the question of building strategic trust, both between the United States and China, but also between China and its neighbors, because the uncertainty and the concerns that China's neighbors and many Americans feel about China's long-term intentions, which, among other things, is fueled both by its problematic behavior with regard to territorial disputes, but also the opacity of its military modernization, represent an impediment to real progress, both in the bilateral relationship, but also in regional growth.

I believe that one of the essential ingredients to developing real trust, as opposed to papering over differences, is direct, high-level dialogue. China is a one-party state, and the ability to speak directly to Chinese leaders is uniquely important. Since taking office, President Obama has met with the Chinese President or the Chinese Premier, I think, something on the order of 19 times, which is extraordinary. But, Secretary Kerry, along with other senior officials, similarly have maintained a very robust rhythm of high-level meetings interspersed, as I mentioned, by telephone calls and so on. And the S&ED, which is 2 weeks out, represents another important vehicle, both for the high-level direct dialogue, but also for the important stakeholders in our respective departments of government and agencies who are working on projects or wrestling with disagreements through the course of the year, to meet in person and to take stock of what they have done, and to chart a program of work ahead for the coming year.

A second area that is essential in building trust, I believe, is promoting people-to-people connections. And through our comprehensive high-level people-to-people dialogue, through our various educational exchanges, through our outreach programs to Chinese citizens and NGOs, and, frankly, through Chinese language training programs for Americans, we are ensuring that the next generation gets a firsthand understanding of what the other culture and the other system is all about.

Thirdly, the economic relationship, as you mentioned, is hugely important. And, as China increasingly develops its own intellectual capital and acquires something worth protecting, we are confident that our messages about the need to protect intellectual property will start to ring true, because the Chinese are suffering both from counterfeit materials, but also from a lack of innovation.

And then, lastly, as I alluded to, greater clarity in China's military modernization will be an important element of creating trust between China and the United States and its neighbors. We have a strong military-to-military dialogue that involves high-level exchanges. The Secretary of Defense has recently been to China. We have got other visits in the works. And we are working hard to remove the uncertainties and the ambiguities in connection with our military-to-military relationship, including by going so far as to include China in some of our multilateral exercises.

Senator CARDIN. Well, thank you very much. I think that gives us an agenda to work on this. It is not easy. I think people-to-people exchanges have been extremely helpful. When I was in China, one of my most enjoyable meetings was with students. It is a country that guards itself pretty carefully when it comes to expression of views. So, I have found students to be very refreshing in that regard. And I think we do have a real challenge on our hands to develop that trust, consistent with our positions on issues, so it is very clear that, for our strategic partnerships to grow, there are areas that need to be understood, and that that comes from the framework that we have two different governments. We understand that. And our goal is to improve that relationship and to make the progress that is important for U.S. interests.

We are going to take—we are going to go to the second panel. Senator Menendez is going to be back in about a moment, so we are going to take a very short recess, and then Senator Menendez will reconvene the committee for the purposes of introducing the second panel.

Ambassador RUSSEL. Thank you very much, Mr. Chairman.

[Recess.]

The CHAIRMAN [presiding]. This hearing will come to order again.

Let me apologize to our witnesses. We have one more vote going on, but I thought that we have probably enough time to listen to both of your testimonies and maybe begin some questioning before we will have to take one more vote and another short recess.

But, we are pleased to be joined by two incredibly important witnesses—J. Stapleton Roy, distinguished scholar and founding director emeritus of the Kissinger Institute on China and the U.S. at the Woodrow Wilson International Center for Scholars, here in Washington; and Dr. Aaron Friedberg, professor of politics and international affairs, at Princeton, which is a university that is in service to the country, but located in the great State of New Jersey. So, we welcome you here.

As I said to our State Department witness, your entire statements will be included in the record. I would ask you to summarize them in about 5 minutes or so, so we could enter into a dialogue.

And we will start with you, Ambassador Roy.

STATEMENT OF HON. J. STAPLETON ROY, DISTINGUISHED SCHOLAR AND FOUNDING DIRECTOR EMERITUS OF THE KISSINGER INSTITUTE ON CHINA AND THE UNITED STATES, WOODROW WILSON INTERNATIONAL CENTER FOR SCHOLARS, WASHINGTON, DC

Ambassador ROY. Thank you, Mr. Chairman, particularly for holding this hearing on an issue which is of vital importance to the United States and to the peace of the world.

The United States, in my judgment, has a sensible and constructive policy framework for dealing with a rising China, but successful implementation of this policy will require patience and perseverance.

East Asian countries worry about U.S. staying power in the region. The United States rebalancing strategy is, in essence, an effort to demonstrate to our friends and allies in East Asia, and to China, that the United States has both the will and the resources to remain actively engaged in East Asia, politically, economically, and militarily, as we regain our economic health.

Fortunately, top leaders in both China and the United States have concluded that unchecked strategic rivalry between the two countries is not in the interests of either.

They have set the strategic goal of striking a stable and sustainable balance between competition and cooperation in the U.S.-China relationship. Accomplishing this will not be easy. A major driver of the growing strategic mistrust between China and the United States is the understandable desire of each side to have a military balance that favors its own interests. This is a natural preference, but it will not contribute to containing strategic rivalry between China and the United States. This is the heart of the strategic problem between the United States and China. We do not know whether a solution can be found, but finding a solution is worth the effort.

In pursuing the goal, both China and the United States are confronted with serious contradictions in our position in the western Pacific. If we do not manage these contradictions properly, the strategic goal of constraining our strategic rivalry will be a vain hope.

In China's case, it must deal with the fundamental contradiction between its commitment to peaceful development and its equally strong commitment to defending China's sovereignty and territorial integrity. If China strays from the path of peaceful development, its hope of achieving the China dream of the great rejuvenation of the Chinese nation will be hopeless.

Adhering to the path of peaceful development is easier said than done, because China is embroiled in territorial disputes with six of its neighbors. An additional aspect of this issue is that domestic influences on China's foreign policy are becoming stronger, limiting China's diplomatic flexibility. This has long been a problem in handling China's relations with Japan, in large measure because domestic attitudes in China toward Japan, and historical memories are so strong, that Chinese leaders must take care not to let the spearhead of nationalism turn against themselves. Historical revisionism in Japan is also a major contributing factor to the current tensions affecting Japan's relations with China and South Korea.

In the case of the South China Sea, domestic influences on China's handling of the issue have become more intense over the last decade, and China's skillful diplomacy in Southeast Asia of a dozen years ago has largely been undone by China's more assertive approach to territorial issues in the South China Sea. China's leaders recognize the problem, and they are giving high-level attention to trying to strengthen China's diplomacy with its neighbors. They had a special conference, in October last year, chaired by Xi Jinping, to address this question. But, China has still not found a satisfactory method of managing this contradiction, and this is contributing to the rise in regional tensions.

In the case of the United States, let me just cite two contradictions in our approach. The first is, the relations between our two allies in Northeast Asia—South Korea and Japan—are not good. They are marked by significant tensions. A second contradiction for the United States is that two of our allies—Japan and the Philippines—are locked in territorial disputes with China over uninhabited islands that are of no interest or importance to the United States. There is no question in my mind that the United States will stand by our allies if they are subjected to aggression, but we do not wish to be dragged into an avoidable conflict with China over small issues, from our standpoint.

For all these reasons, we cannot be complacent in looking to the future, although I think there are grounds for optimism that we can actually handle these problems and steer them in the right direction.

There are troublesome negative aspects in our bilateral relations with China that, if not handled correctly, could increase regional tensions and damage the interests of both countries. We have not yet been able to stabilize the balance between cooperation and competition in the relationship.

In the United States, the sharp increases in China's defense spending, beginning in the mid-1990s, are feeding concerns that China poses a potential threat to the United States position in the Asia-Pacific. In my view, conventional diplomacy will not be sufficient to limit and hopefully reverse our strategic rivalry with China.

It is the normal responses of human nature that have led to confrontations throughout history, and we can see this pattern unfolding in the crisis in Europe over Ukraine and in the rising tensions between China and Japan. This is normal behavior. You do something I do not like; I respond with actions that you do not like. And you have this back-and-forth. This is the reason why rising powers have more often than not gotten into confrontation with established powers.

It was unconventional behavior on the part of China and the United States 42 years ago that achieved the breakthrough in our relations that led to the establishment of U.S.-PRC diplomatic relations. Similarly, it took a leader of Deng Xiaoping's courage and foresight to state, 35 years ago, that territorial problems between China and Japan are too complicated for the current generation to resolve, and should be left for future generations to resolve. By taking that unconventional position, Deng greatly facilitated the positive development of Sino-Japanese relations over the next quarter century. We need to be equally daring in our approach to stabilizing our relations with China.

In conclusion, let me stress that China's economic rise has benefited China's neighbors and the region as a whole. All of China's neighbors have an interest in continuing economic cooperation with China and do not support a containment strategy that would divide the region. Their interest is in responsible Chinese behavior as a major emerging power, not in constraining China's growth. When China, in their eyes, behaves irresponsibly or seems ready to act coercively, they want the assurance provided by the reliable presence of a militarily strong country, such as the United States, that can offset Chinese growing power.

At the same time, no regional country wants to be forced to choose between China and the United States. If the United States, in regional eyes, seems to be mishandling its relations with China in ways that make China a more nationalistic or dangerous neighbor, confidence in the United States regional role decreases.

In short, our skill in dealing with China is directly linked to how successful we will be in retaining the confidence of our friends and allies in East Asia. This is a healthy dynamic. It rewards responsible behavior on the part of both China and the United States, and it creates disincentives for irresponsible behavior. This is important, because the central purpose of U.S. policy in East Asia is to have a positive and constructive relationship with China.

Thank you.

The CHAIRMAN. Thank you very much.

Dr. Friedberg.

STATEMENT OF DR. AARON L. FRIEDBERG, PROFESSOR OF POLITICS AND INTERNATIONAL AFFAIRS, PRINCETON UNIVERSITY, PRINCETON, NJ

Dr. FRIEDBERG. Thank you very much, Senators. It is an honor for me to have this opportunity to express my views.

The relationship between the United States and China is clearly mixed. It contains elements of cooperation as well as competition. In my view, the areas of cooperation are less impressive and less substantial than is sometimes claimed, while the sources of competition are deeper and more profound than many prefer to believe.

I think that the current and emerging competition between the United States and China is not the result of misperception or misunderstanding. And, unfortunately, I do not believe that it will be alleviated by dialogue or high-level meetings, as important as these may be.

The competitive aspects of the relationship, in my view, spring instead from two deep sources. First are the classic dynamics of great-power politics. China is a rising power. Rising powers, historically, have wanted to assert themselves to reshape the rules, the institutions, and sometimes the territorial boundaries that were put into place when they were relatively weak.

A second factor, which, in my view, is important, but does not always get the attention it deserves, is ideology. We often hear it said that China is no longer a Communist country, and therefore, there is no basis for ideological friction or mistrust between China and the United States. While it may be true that China's leaders are no longer Marxists, they are still Leninists, by which I mean they continue to be committed to one-party rule, and they regard the United States and other democratic countries as posing an existential threat to their regime. It is in part for this reason that they want to push back American's presence and influence in Asia.

As regards the future of United States-China relations, in my view, if China's power continues to grow, but if it continues to be ruled by a one-party authoritarian regime, the competitive aspects of the relationship are going to grow, while the areas of cooperation are going to dwindle. I should say I do not think this means that conflict between the two countries is inevitable. I do not believe that is the case. But, I am afraid that the risks of conflict will grow. And indeed, this is precisely what appears to be happening today.

In the past 5 years, China has used stronger, more strident language and more assertive and, at times, forceful actions to assert its claims to control the waters and airspace off its eastern seaboard. Chinese spokesmen and some Western analysts have sought to deny that any shift has taken place or to explain those changes that have occurred as mere reactions to the behavior of others, or as the byproduct of competition among bureaucracies, or the unauthorized actions of a handful of rogue PLA officers, or a reflexive response to popular nationalist pressures.

With the passage of time, it seems to me that these claims have become increasingly difficult to sustain. Beijing's recent behavior appears to be deliberate, purposeful, and coordinated, but it suggests an adjustment in tactics and time lines rather than a fundamental shift in strategy. China appears to be pushing harder to achieve its long-standing goals of expanding its own regional power and influence while constricting the power, influence, and position of the United States. In the long run, Beijing evidently hopes to displace the United States and to restore China to what it regards as its rightful place as the preponderant power in the Asia-Pacific region.

In addition to advancing its claims to control most of the water and resources off its coasts, Beijing is using calibrated threats in an attempt to intimidate its neighbors, to demonstrate the inadequacy of U.S. security guarantees, and, if possible, to drive wedges between the United States and some of its regional friends and allies.

China's increased assertiveness, I think, reflects a mix of arrogance and insecurity. Since the onset of the global financial crisis in 2008–2009, many Chinese analysts and policymakers have concluded that the United States has entered into a period of unexpectedly rapid decline in its power and influence. Chinese planners appear to have concluded that, at least for the next several years, the United States will continue to be strategically preoccupied and financially constrained, and that, if they play their cards right during this period, they may be able to create facts and consolidate their position.

But, this near-term confidence, I think, is mixed with longer term concern. Among other factors, slower economic growth and continuing revelations about the extent and depth of official corruption could threaten internal stability and regime survival. A more assertive stance may enable Beijing to achieve victories that contribute to its proclaimed goal of "national rejuvenation" and enhance the CCP's legitimacy by casting it as the defender of China's honor and greatness. Regardless of the results, however, the regime appears to believe that an atmosphere of increased tension and friction with foreign rivals can help it to rally support and deflect possible public resentment from its own inadequacies and failings.

China's recent actions are deliberately dangerous. Its leaders are manipulating risk, or playing chicken. They are knowingly creating hazardous situations, in the hopes that others will back down. I think there is an element of bluff, here. I do not think China's leaders seek armed conflict. They certainly do not seek it with the United States. And, as a result, I think that, if faced with a firm response, they are likely to adopt a more cautious stance. Nevertheless, even if it is not intended to do so, the kind of behavior in which they are presently engaged could all too easily lead to confrontation and escalation.

In the long run, China's assertiveness may turn out to be counterproductive and even self-defeating. If its Asian neighbors respond by increasing their own capabilities and working more closely with one another and with the United States, they may be able to block Beijing's initiatives and balance its power. But, such an outcome is not automatic or inevitable. In the absence of an effective American response, China may yet be able to successfully pursue a divide-and-conquer strategy, intimidating some of its neighbors into acquiescence while isolating and demoralizing others. Indeed, this appears to be what Beijing is attempting to do: reaching out to Washington, proclaiming its desire for a new type great-power relationship with the United States, while at the same time ratcheting up pressure on some key targets, especially United States allies—Japan and the Philippines, as well Vietnam.

Just very briefly on the question of an American response. For most of the last two decades, the United States has pursued a mixed strategy toward China, seeking to engage it through trade, diplomacy, people-to-people contact, and so on, while at the same time taking steps to preserve a favorable balance of power in East Asia, even as China grows stronger. In my view, it is neither feasible nor, at this point, necessary to abandon this mixed strategy in favor of something radically different. What is required instead is a readjustment of the blending of the two elements; and, in particular, an increased emphasis on the balancing portion of America's strategic portfolio.

The current administration began to move in this direction in 2011, with its announcement of a pivot toward Asia. But, its efforts to date have been, and I think are widely perceived in the region to be, inadequate. There is growing concern on the part of friends and allies that, despite the rhetoric of its leaders, the United States may lack the resources, the focus, and perhaps the resolve necessary to withstand Chinese pressure and sustain a position of leadership.

A variety of measures, I think, are necessary in order to counteract this. I would just emphasize two themes. On the one hand, I think it is necessary for the United States and its allies to take steps that impose some costs on China for its more assertive behavior. And, on the other, it is essential for us to increase the capacity of our allies, as well as our own, to deter and, if necessary, to defeat attempts at coercion. Among the various steps that are needed, I think one in particular stands out, and it is a long-term problem. The United States has to develop, articulate, and fund, together with its allies, a military strategy that will enable it to continue to project power into the western Pacific under any circumstances and despite the ongoing deployment by China of so-called antiaccess area denial capabilities.

Our position in Asia is built on our alliances, and those, in turn, rest on assurances that we will come to the aid of our allies if they are threatened or attacked. Without an effective and timely response, Beijing's ongoing military buildup will begin to call the credibility of our assurances into question, and this could weaken our alliances, increase the risk of aggression, and potentially endanger the peace and stability of the entire Asia-Pacific region.

Thank you.

[The prepared statement of Dr. Friedberg follows:]

PREPARED STATEMENT OF AARON L. FRIEDBERG

INTRODUCTION

In the past 5 years China has used stronger, more strident language and more assertive, and at times, forceful actions to assert its claims to control the waters and air space off its eastern seaboard. Chinese spokesmen (and some Western analysts) have sought to deny that any shift has taken place, or to explain those changes that have occurred as mere reactions to the behavior of others. With the passage of time such claims have become increasingly difficult to sustain.

Examples of China's growing assertiveness continue to multiply. The most recent include Beijing's unilateral declaration of an Air Defense Identification Zone that covers Japanese-controlled islands in the East China Sea in November of last year, the deliberate near-collision of a PLAN vessel with the U.S. Navy cruiser *Cowpens* in December and, in the past 2 months, the deployment of oil rigs and a small armada of naval and maritime patrol vessels into waters claimed by Vietnam.

These developments raise three questions:

—What explains Beijing's increased assertiveness?
—What are the likely implications of this behavior for China's relations with its neighbors and with the United States?
—And how should the U.S. respond?

Explaining increased Chinese assertiveness

With the end of the cold war, China began to pursue a consistent and generally cautious strategy for dealing with its neighbors and with the United States. This strategy reflected the wisdom of former party chief Deng Xiaoping who, in the wake of the Tiananmen Square massacre, the fall of the Berlin Wall and the U.S. defeat of Iraq in the first Persian Gulf war advised his colleagues that China should "hide its capabilities and bide its time."

At least until recently Chinese strategy has evidently been governed by three axioms:

—"Avoid confrontation" (especially with the United States, but also with China's wealthy and powerful neighbors).

—"Build 'comprehensive national power' " (a concept Chinese analysts use to refer to all of the various dimensions and instruments of national capability).

—"Advance incrementally."

Regarding this last point: Chinese policymakers assessed that they were in a relatively weak position and needed time to build their strength, but they did not believe that they could or should remain passive. To the contrary, over the last two decades they have sought opportunities to enhance their country's influence and strengthen its position, while simultaneously attempting to erode and constrict those of the United States. The ultimate aims of Chinese strategy appear to be two-fold:

—To preserve the Chinese Communist Party's monopoly on domestic political power.

—To displace the United States and restore China to its rightful place as the preponderant power in East Asia.

Beijing's recent behavior suggests an adjustment in tactics and timelines rather than a fundamental shift in strategy. China is pushing harder to achieve its long-standing goals. In addition to advancing its claims to control most of the water and resources off its coasts, it is using calibrated threats in an attempt to intimidate its neighbors, demonstrate the inadequacy of U.S. security guarantees, and, if possible, to drive wedges between the United States and some of its regional friends and allies.

China's increased assertiveness reflects a mix of arrogance and insecurity. Following the onset of the global financial crisis, many Chinese analysts and policymakers concluded that the United States had entered into a period of unexpectedly rapid decline in its relative power and influence. With their country's fortunes seemingly on the rise, some argued that the time had come for China, if not to abandon "hiding and biding," then at least to adopt a more forward-leaning posture in its dealings with the rest of the world. Chinese planners appear to have concluded that, at least for the next several years, the United States will continue to be strategically preoccupied and fiscally constrained. If it plays its cards right during this period, China can "create facts" and consolidate its position.

Near term confidence is mixed with longer term concern. Among other factors, slower economic growth and continuing revelations about the extent and depth of official corruption could threaten internal stability and regime survival. A more assertive stance may enable Beijing to achieve victories that contribute to "national rejuvenation" and enhance the CCP's legitimacy by casting it as the defender of China's honor and greatness. Regardless of the results, however, the regime appears to believe that an atmosphere of increased tension and friction with foreign rivals can help it to rally support and deflect possible public resentment from its own inadequacies and failings.

Implications for regional peace and stability

China's recent actions are deliberately dangerous. Its leaders are manipulating risk or playing "chicken"; they are knowingly creating hazardous situations in the hope that others will back down. Even if it is not intended to do so, such behavior could easily lead to confrontation and escalation.

In the long run, China's assertiveness could also turn out to be counterproductive and even self-defeating. If its Asian nations respond by increasing their own capabilities and working more closely with one another and with the United States they may be able to block Beijing's initiatives and balance its power. But such an outcome is not automatic or inevitable. In the absence of an effective American response, China may yet be able to successfully pursue a divide and conquer strategy: intimidating some of its neighbors into acquiescence while isolating and demoralizing others. Indeed, this appears to be precisely what Beijing is now trying to do: reaching out to Washington and proclaiming its desire to form a "new type great power relationship" with the United States, while at the same time ratcheting up pressure on key targets, especially U.S. allies Japan and the Philippines, as well as Vietnam.

How should the U.S. respond?

For most of the last two decades the United States, like China, has been pursuing an essentially constant strategy. Despite occasional shifts in emphasis, successive administrations have sought to engage China, primarily through trade and diplomacy, while at the same time taking steps to preserve a favorable balance of power in East Asia. In addition to maintaining and selectively strengthening its own military capabilities, Washington has sought to bolster relations with its traditional treaty allies and to build quasi-alliance relationships with other countries (including Singapore and India) that share its concerns about the possible implications of China's growing strength.

The objectives of U.S. strategy have been, first, to "tame" China by giving it a stake in the preservation of the existing international order and second, in the long run, to transform it, encouraging the evolution of its domestic political system away from authoritarianism and toward something more closely resembling liberal democracy.

It is neither feasible nor, at this point, necessary to abandon this mixed strategy in favor of something different. What is required, instead, is a readjustment of the blending of the two elements and, in particular, an increased emphasis on the balancing portion of America's strategic portfolio. The current administration began to move in this direction in 2011 with its announcement of a "pivot" toward Asia (later renamed the "rebalance"), but its efforts to date have been, and are widely perceived in the region to be, inadequate. There is growing concern on the part of friends and allies that, despite the rhetoric of its leaders, the United States may lack the resources, the focus, and perhaps the resolve necessary to sustain a position of leadership.

Among the measures that will be needed to alleviate these fears, one in particular stands out. The United States must develop, articulate fund and (together with its allies) implement a military strategy that will enable it to continue to project power into the Western Pacific, under any circumstances, and despite the ongoing deployment by China of so-called antiaccess/area denial capabilities. America's position in Asia is built on its alliances and those, in turn, rest on assurances that it will come to the aid of its allies if they are threatened or attacked. Without an effective and timely response, Beijing's ongoing military buildup will begin to call the credibility of those assurances into question, weakening U.S. alliances, increasing the risk of aggression, and potentially endangering the peace and stability of the entire Asia-Pacific region.

The CHAIRMAN. Well, thank you both.

I have let you both go over time because you had a lot of good things to say, insights, which will mean that we are going to have to take a brief recess. We have one final vote. I think we will—Senator Corker and I both know how we are voting. We will come right back, and we will get into a line of questioning, because you have raised many issues beyond the questions I originally had.

So, this committee will stand in recess, subject to the call of the Chair.

[Recess.]

The CHAIRMAN. This hearing will come back to order.

Thank you both for your forbearance.

You have both raised some very interesting points. So, let me ask you both. China: strategic competitor? Strategic rival? Strategic problem? Ever, potentially, a strategic ally?

Ambassador ROY. All of the above.

The CHAIRMAN. I was afraid that was going to be your answer.

Ambassador ROY. No, seriously. I was, for 45 years, a U.S. Foreign Service officer, and spent 9 years working on the Soviet Union, and even longer than that dealing with China during periods when it was a hostile country and during periods when it was a friendly country and we were expanding our relations rapidly. Elements of cooperation and of competition are inherently part of relations between major powers. And certainly China is a major power. I do not think that getting rid of strategic rivalry between the United States and China is a realistic approach to the relationship.

But, calibrating the balance between cooperation on common interests and the rivalry elements that are part of major-power relations is what diplomacy is all about. And it does not, and should not, drive us in the direction of conflict if we can stabilize the strategic rivalry. The reason why we talk about trying to create this new type of bilateral relationship is because, if you do not constrain the strategic rivalry, it can drive you in the wrong direction and result in hostile rivalry, which returns you to a negative cold war type of relationship, which we are far away from in our relationship with China.

The CHAIRMAN. Dr. Friedberg, I would like to hear from you, too. And one of the things that you said in your testimony, that I noted, was that this mixed strategy that we have—that maybe what we need is an adjustment, I think you said, of the blending. And can you speak to the overarching question I just asked Ambassador Roy, as well as—well, what is the blend—what should the blending look like?

Dr. FRIEDBERG. As far as whether China's a competitor, a rival, a problem, and so on, I think it is all of those things. I think we have to acknowledge the extent to which, in fact, there is this competitive or rivalrous component to the relationship. And I do not think we have always been as candid as we need to be in acknowledging that fact. For reasons that I indicated, I think the competitive aspects of the relationship are growing in intensity. I agree with Ambassador Roy that part of our objective should be to contain that and prevent that from spilling over and contaminating and coloring the entire relationship.

I do not think it is inevitable that China and the United States need to be in a zero-sum relationship, enemies in the ways that the United States and the Soviet Union were during the cold war. But I also do not see much prospect for anything resembling an alliance or a genuine deep partnership between the United States and China for the foreseeable future.

As far as the mixing of elements, in our strategy, with all of the debates about our policy, since the end of the cold war at least, in fact, both Republican and Democratic administrations have pursued a broadly similar strategy for dealing with China, and it has had these two components: engagement—obviously, the diplomatic part of the engagement goes all the way back to the late 1960s and early 1970s; the economic piece has become much more important, clearly, since the early 1990s.

But, at the same time, I would say, from the mid-1990s onward, successive administrations have also sought deliberately to strengthen our position in the region to maintain a balance of power that is favorable to us and to our friends. And we have done that in three ways. One is by maintaining and strengthening our own military capabilities in the region. So, the pivot, in that sense, is not new; it really goes back to the Clinton administration. We have also tried to strengthen and build on our traditional alliance relationships, particularly with Japan, Korea, and Australia. And we have also developed what I would call quasi-alliance relationships with other countries in the region to whom we do not extend security guarantees, but who share with us, to some degree, a concern about the growth of Chinese power, including a small country like Singapore, and a very large one like India.

What has happened over time is that we have modulated that blend, or changed that mix of elements. When the current administration first came into office during its first couple of years, it sought to play up engagement with China, as with Russia, and to downplay the balancing part of the formula. Since 2011, I think, in response to increased Chinese assertiveness, the Obama administration has sought to increase the balancing piece of the portfolio. I think they were correct to do that. My concern is that they have had difficulty in following through.

The CHAIRMAN. Let me ask you—so, Ambassador Roy, you talked about patience, that it will require patience. And I often hear this when I travel in the region, when I speak to regional leaders who come here. I often hear about this element of patience. And I understand that. Except—or maybe you can help me and the committee understand how—as we exhibit patience, how do we also deal with issues like the intellectual property rights issue, the counterfeit issue, the cyber theft issue, currency manipulation? Those are all economic elements of this competition, even though those elements are not, obviously, legitimate—in international norms, legitimate competition.

And so, how do we press those issues? How do we press issues about right of freedom of passage, navigation in the South China Sea? How do we press our—I hope, our human rights issues, even though I think we have increasingly been reluctant to do that? We do it, but it seems to me it is—the tier is all the way down there, in terms of pursuing human rights issues, whether it be in China or the way they treat Tibet.

For both of you, give me a sense of how, as we engage, do we at the same time robustly pursue the very essence of this competition that we hope to be in in a more legitimate international way, when there are hundreds of thousands of jobs being lost in the United States, billions of dollars being lost. Patience has, obviously, its limitations.

Ambassador ROY. It is a very good question. And it is one of the frustrating——

The CHAIRMAN. We only ask good questions here at the committee. [Laughter.]

Ambassador ROY. Well——

The CHAIRMAN. No, it is not—that is not—I would like to think that is true, but it is humorous, if nothing else. But——

Ambassador ROY. When you would like to see changes in other countries, where you have only a very limited ability to actually force them to make the changes you would like to see, you need to have patience, and you need to understand the processes that would be most effective in accomplishing this.

And, frankly, one of the reasons why I was comfortable representing a country that takes a high profile on human rights issues is because our high profile on human rights issues is a function of the fact that, from the beginning of our republic, we had built-in violations of human rights that were fundamental. We had slavery embedded in our Constitution. For 70 years, we tried to solve it through a political process. We failed. We fought a bloody civil war, and then we reinstituted Jim Crow laws that persisted for nearly 100 more years.

When I was Ambassador in China, we created a linkage between human rights in China and most-favored-nations treatment and wanted fundamental improvements in seven areas of human rights in 1 year. Well, if the United States takes centuries to deal with fundamental human rights problems, why do we expect that other countries can deal with them overnight? So, that is why I say we need patience.

Now, I have also reflected on this. If other countries had set the goal during the 19th century of forcing the United States to give up slavery, would it have been helpful? What actions would they have taken? Well, in fact, I think there were some factors that influenced us. For example, Britain eliminated slavery. So, in other words, some countries were setting a behavior pattern which actually influenced thinking in the United States. I have found that the power of example is much more useful in dealing with other countries on human rights issues, or on intellectual property protection issues than simply haranguing them about it.

Now, on the intellectual property issue, the reality is, the countries that produce intellectual property are the ones most devoted to protecting it. And countries that do not produce intellectual property tend to think that theft of intellectual property is in their national interest.

When I was a diplomat in the Republic of China on Taiwan, back in the 1960s, they were defiant on piracy issues. For example, they said, ''Your textbooks are too expensive for us. We are a developing country; therefore we are going to steal them, and too bad.'' And that is the way they behaved. And it took us decades to force a friendly government to begin to respect our intellectual property interests. So, that was an example of a country that was determined simply to act in its own interest, because, at the time, it was not producing intellectual property.

Now, one of the reasons why I am optimistic, in the long term, about China's moving toward greater respect for protection of intellectual property is because, unlike some of the countries I have served in, China has big ambitions about becoming a creator of intellectual property. And if you create intellectual property, you cannot do so effectively if you do not protect it.

I have had meals with Chinese movie producers who described the types of movies they could produce and the ones they could not produce. And the ones they could not produce were the ones that could be easily ripped off inside China. They could not make any money, and therefore they simply did not produce those types of movies. But, in other areas, there were better protections, and therefore they could move ahead.

So, I have discovered, in dealing at the highest levels of the Chinese Government, there is an intellectual understanding of the importance of protecting intellectual property, but it is a country that, historically, in modern history, has not produced much intellectual property, and therefore, there is a habit of ripping off intellectual property from others.

I recall 10 years ago, when we began to clamp down on downloading free music from the Internet, that our college students were all busy ripping off intellectual property. And we began to tighten the screws on them, and I think it is been substantially improved. But, in the process, our young people continued to think they had some——

The CHAIRMAN. Yes. But——

Ambassador ROY [continuing]. Right to——

The CHAIRMAN [continuing]. We did something about it.

Ambassador ROY. We did something about it.

The CHAIRMAN. And that is a—one of the fundamental——

Ambassador ROY. Well, I think we are actually making progress in this area. And if you talk to Microsoft and some of the other countries that have—companies that have been working on this, long term, it is not that there has not been progress; it is simply there has not been enough. And therefore, they are continuing to push ahead, and I think that the U.S. Government has to support those efforts.

The CHAIRMAN. Let me turn to my colleagues.

Senator Corker.

Senator CORKER. Thank you, Mr. Chairman.

Ambassador, Doctor, thank you both for being here.

We had a group of Chinese businessmen here a couple of years ago, and I made some comments to them and used the word ''competition'' among other kinds of things, and then realized, in talking with them, that they do not view us that way at all. Now, these were businessmen.

If we were having this same kind of hearing in China, and they had two witnesses that were talking about the United States, how do they view us? How does the citizenry generally view us? I know that is very diverse, with that many people. And how does the government actually view the United States? We look at them as competition, we look at them as a growing threat. Those are some of the words that you all have used. How do they view us?

Dr. FRIEDBERG. Well, of course, as you indicate, it is a country of 1.3 billion people——

Senator CORKER. Yes.

Dr. FRIEDBERG [continuing]. So there are a lot of——

Senator CORKER. Yes.

Dr. FRIEDBERG [continuing]. Different opinions, although they do not all have the opportunity to be expressed because——

Senator CORKER. Yes.

Dr. FRIEDBERG [continuing]. Of the character of the Chinese political regime. I think the Chinese strategic elites, so the people who worry about China's strategy and about the United States in particular, do see the United States as a strategic competitor, as a threat to China's interests. As I indicated, they believe that, for ideological reasons, the United States is fundamentally opposed to their current regime, seeks to encircle them, to block them from achieving their rightful place in the world, potentially to destabilize them from within, and so on.

So, I think there is a deep-seated suspicion of the United States. And, in part, I believe that is one of the reasons that Chinese leaders and strategists want to extend their influence in the region and would like to see the influence and presence of the United States diminish, because they see us as threatening.

Throughout this broader swath of Chinese society, I think there is a much wider range of views. People in business see many opportunities, of course, in dealing with the United States. I see many Chinese students coming to the United States and studying. And, in many cases, they are very enthusiastic about American culture and society and so on.

Senator CORKER. But, the people who make the decisions and, therefore, set the policy, see us the same way we see them.

Dr. FRIEDBERG. Well, I think it is even darker. I think they really—as I said, I think they really believe that we want to——

Senator CORKER. Yes.

Dr. FRIEDBERG [continuing]. Contain and bring them down.

Senator CORKER. Yes.

And you agree with that, Ambassador?

Ambassador ROY. I think that represents one aspect of it. But, there is a very strong different aspect to it. China's big goal, the China dream, is to modernize China. Chinese leaders at the very top recognize that they will greatly slow the process of modernization of China if they do not have good relations with modern countries. So that, going way back to the 1980s, when we established diplomatic relations, China has attached high importance to improving and sustaining relations with the modern countries of the world. These are the countries to whom they sent the students that they needed to get educated to bring back the skills that were part of the modernization process. And I still encounter an understanding of the importance of that factor. It is a stabilizing factor in a highly competitive relationship between the United States and China. China still wants good relations with the United States, because, otherwise, the Chinese dream is a fading chimera that they will never get closer to unless they are able to maintain the close relations with modern countries.

But, modern countries have modern ideas. And what is significant, for somebody like me—who served in China as a U.S. Government official from 1978 to 1981, and then was there as Ambassador, and now I visit it—is the whole nature of thinking in China about political change, about government structures, has changed over the last 30–40 years, because all of a sudden, at every level of Chinese society—in the government, in the educational institutions, in the business community—you have people who have been educated in the West. They do not see our system as something that can be transplanted to China, but they understand that, in dealing with corruption, a free press can be helpful. Can China really address corruption within the Communist Party if it has a judicial system that is controlled by the Communist Party? So, already you are beginning to see different language coming in.

If you look at the language of the Third Plenum Communique that came out in November of last year, all of a sudden they are talking about rule by law, because the corruption is when officials do not abide by the laws that are on the books, but simply arbitrarily exercise their power. And they are talking about having checks and balances on the exercise of power. Well, this is something that we addressed back in the Federalist papers in the 18th century. And yet, that type of discourse about exercising power in the sunlight, having the people serve as a check on the exercise of power, putting power in a cage so that it cannot be arbitrarily used, all of this is language taken from that Third Plenum document that emerged last November. You did not find these concepts part of the discourse in China before.

So, this is how countries change. They have exposure to different societies. The modern ones are the ones that influence them most. And then they begin to borrow from those societies, and gradually you find that they are talking about issues in a different way.

Again, I emphasize one other point. China's the only authoritarian country in the world which has age limits on their senior leaders. China's top leaders are expected to step down around the age of 70. We have had Presidential candidates who were near the age of 70. In China, you cannot have that. And they have put a two-term limit in effect, which means that the top leaders can only serve 10 years. And the replacements have to be 10 years younger or they will be over the age limits at the end of the period.

So, one of the advantages of a democratic system of government is that we can change leaders, and changing leaders is often the only way that you can change bad policies. But, now China has generational shifts that are also built into a regular process of changing leaders, so that when we get the next change of leadership in China, in 2022, the people will be under 60 years old who take the top positions. They will have no memories of the cultural revolution. They will have spent their entire lives, adult lives, under conditions of reform and openness, with ready access to the outside world.

Do we really expect that those leaders are going to use the same types of governance concepts inside China that the old generation, that was not university-educated, or, if they were educated, it was in Russia, or the Soviet Union, back in the 1950s? No. That is not the way humans behave. People reflect the experiences they have as part of their maturing process. And the experiences that the last 30 years of Chinese have had are radically different from the experiences they had before China opened itself up to the outside world.

But, we are talking about change over a period of decades, and that is why I talk about the need for patience and perseverance in dealing with China.

Senator CORKER. If I can ask just one more question.

The age issue you mentioned certainly would wreck the United States Senate. [Laughter.]

The CHAIRMAN. Present company excluded.

Senator CORKER. That is right. [Laughter.]

So, it is understandable to see why you would undertake, from their perspective, cyber theft. It is enriching them. They can move ahead decades quickly by ripping us off. You can understand that counterfeiting and all of those things. Again, it is not proper, but, it is in their interests to rip us and other countries off to pursue a more rapid growth there. And it is unfortunate that they condone that. And I realize, over time, as you mentioned, that may well change as they develop their own.

If they view us as a threat, and they view us as competition, what is in their national interest, relative to the silly disputes that are taking place in the South and East China Sea, which immediately, as you all mentioned in your earlier testimony, provokes a response, "They do something; we do something"? How is that, again, in their overall strategic interest to cause us to want to engage more fully in that way because of their breaking of international norms?

Dr. FRIEDBERG. Well, if I could start by just saying something on the previous issue, because I think it is related, I will give you the glass-half-empty view. It seems to me that the Chinese regime, although it has evolved and changed, and Chinese society has changed in many ways, maintains its commitment to the preservation of one-party rule. Its interest in reform is not rooted in principle so much as in practicality and a desire to maintain its control. And it has proven to be quite smart, sophisticated, but also ruthless in suppressing dissent and maintaining the dominance of the CCP. I think there is an anxiety on the part of the leadership about the future, for reasons that I suggested. And the ways in which the regime has sought to bolster its legitimacy, particularly since the decline of the appeal, such as it was, of Marxist-Leninist ideology, has been to emphasize economic growth and improvements in welfare, but also, increasingly, nationalism and this idea of a Chinese rejuvenation, the great Chinese dream, and so on.

So, these disputes, although they appear to be over insignificant pieces of rock, actually are potentially extremely important, and I think, from the point of view of the regime, may be useful, or they may see them as being useful, as a way of rallying and mobilizing popular support behind the government and deflecting frustration and resentments outward against historic rivals, like Japan, and, to some degree, the United States.

These disputes are about resources and about who is going to be the dominant power in the region. China is seeking to establish itself in that position, in part by forcing others to give way in the face of its pressure. But, I do think that these disputes have an internal function, and it is related to the regime's concern about maintaining domestic control.

So, yes, in the long run, I hope that Ambassador Roy is right and that we have this peaceful evolution, but, in the shorter term, I am concerned that the regime, in its efforts to maintain its control, may be undertaking dangerous and aggressive external policies.

The CHAIRMAN. Senator Rubio.

Senator RUBIO. Thank you.

I wanted to return to this notion of—Secretary Russel, about—you used this term, "the China dream," which I have heard used to describe the situation in China, their ambitions for their country. As it is been described to me in my visits to—in my visit to Asia, and by others since—and there might be some dispute about it—but, they view the China dream—they describe it as follows: that China views itself, from a historical perspective, as the world's great power, that they view the last 150 years as an aberration in world history, and they are simply now reemerging into their rightful place. And "their rightful place" means not simply displacing the U.S. as a dominant power in the region, but, in fact, in some—in many respects, behaving like the dominant power, vis-a-vis their neighbors and the way they act toward their neighbors. I think that is further compounded by what is no doubt over the last 10 years not just a massive expansion in their military capabilities, but by increasing assertiveness, for example, in their claims in the areas within the nine-dash line, their territorial claims, and potentially their claims on navigation rights, which is something that we should care about deeply.

You described it as simply a desire to modernize the country, but others have described it as much more—much deeper than simply that, that, in fact—and perhaps you discussed this earlier, but that the China dream, in fact, is about establishing themselves as the world's dominant power in a zero-sum game with the United States and the established institutions under the post-World War II world. What is the right way to view their mindset and—so that we can understand better some of the policy decisions they are making?

Ambassador ROY. It needs to be viewed in its historical context in order to have some idea of what they are talking about. The two words that have generally characterized the goals of China's reformers, going back to the Qing Dynasty in the late 19th century, have been wealth and power. This was what they wanted China to recapture. China used to be a country that had wealth and power, and then it lost it during its period of decline and exploitation by more powerful countries.

And so, right up through the 20th century, the goal has been restoring China's wealth and power. That is not a bad goal. All countries, in a sense, aspire to it. But, there are aspects of it which are dangerous. And one aspect of it that I find particularly disturbing is in the documents coming out of the 18th Party Congress, which was 2 years ago, in talking about why China needed powerful armed forces. They did not simply relate them to the defense needs of the country and to the economic development needs of the country, protecting their economic development. They said they needed powerful armed forces commensurate with the country's international standing. That is a very dangerous concept. It means that China is now saying, "We need powerful armed forces because we are emerging as a great power."

And this represents a type of great-power chauvinism which I think is inherently dangerous. I cannot get anybody else to pay attention to what I see as a very dangerous phraseology emerging in that document. When I discuss it with my China colleagues, you know, they do not pay much attention to that phrase. But, to me, it is very disturbing. What does it mean for China to have powerful armed forces commensurate with its international standing? When its economy overtakes that of the United States, which might occur in the near future, does that mean they need armed forces that are bigger than those of the United States?

So, in other words, I see two sides of this. I see a China which has legitimate aspirations to restore its wealth and power, and I see a China which also may have the typical ambitions of somebody who is getting strong enough to be the big bully in the block.

Senator RUBIO. I guess, from their actions, though, you can deduce the following. I think this is a safe statement, and you are certainly an expert on this, so I am glad we have the opportunity to talk to you about it. Since the end of World War II especially, we have had an established international order that involves resolving disputes through mediation and other methods——

Ambassador ROY. Right.

Senator RUBIO [continuing]. And so forth. There is been an economic order, as well, involving all sorts of things, from trade to currencies. And what I take from the actions I have seen recently is, the Chinese attitude toward this is, ''We did not write these rules, we did not participate in their creation. They were written in a way to benefit the West or others, and we do not necessarily feel like we need to comply with them. In fact, we would like to reorder or rewrite, to some extent, by changing facts on the ground, in some instances, how all of this operates, moving forward. And as a rising power, we intend to do so.'' And that includes, by the way, increasing, not just their military capacity, but their willingness to use that capacity, at least now, to various different means to assert their territorial claims. So, in fact, they are not just—this is not just a rhetorical——

Ambassador ROY. Right.

Senator RUBIO [continuing]. Challenge that they pose. We are beginning to see this reflected in the actions that they are taking.

Ambassador ROY. This gets into the question of whether China's a status-quo power or whether it is trying to overthrow the status quo and establish a new one. I actually find that the truth, as I see it, is that China is somewhere in between that. And common sense tells you that when a new power emerges into an existing system, the existing system has to make certain accommodations. And if the system will not make the accommodations, then the rising power will want to change the system.

But, in fact, the existing system is accommodating China to a significant degree, but not to a 100-percent degree. So, for example, China sees the World Bank and the Asian Development Bank as largely controlled by Western countries and, in the case of the Asian Development Bank, by Japan. And so, they are talking about setting up an Asia Infrastructure Investment Bank, which will be largely funded by billions of dollars from China and which will engage in reconstructing a new Silk Road. In other words, they will engage in infrastructure projects leading into Central Asia and the Middle East. So, they are thinking big in these terms.

But, this is not the same, to me, as being anti-status-quo. It simply means that China wants more accommodation for its interests, and the question of whether we can maintain the stability of the international system is partly the degree to which China will accommodate itself to the existing institutions and the degree to which the existing institutions will accommodate themselves to the fact that China has growing stature in the world, has growing financial resources, it swings more weight in the world. It is now a giant factor in international trade, which is one of the reasons why our Transpacific Partnership has the door open for China to participate. Because what would be the sense of having a transpacific partnership in which the country that has the largest trade relationships with the countries that are members of the partnership is not within it?

Senator RUBIO. I guess that my final question is, Is it fair to say that, among leading policymakers within the Communist Party in

China, they view international relations as a zero-sum game, that, in order for them to increase, someone else has to decrease? Is that——

Ambassador ROY. No. In fact, who am I to say what their secret thoughts are? But, I have not encountered that view in any of the senior-level conversations that I have been privileged to be part of.

Senator RUBIO. So, what about this, then? Is it fair to say that there are commentators or others within—and others close to the decisionmaking process—that view the United States as a declining power and China as a rising power?

Ambassador ROY. I would say that is almost a universal perception in China, at the moment.

Senator RUBIO. Universal, meaning——

Ambassador ROY. But, it is not just——

Senator RUBIO [continuing]. Among their political leadership?

Ambassador ROY. I encounter that perception in Korea, in Japan, in Southeast Asia, and in Europe. In other words, I think there is a very dangerous perception out that the United States is a declining power because of the fact that we have not recovered in a robust fashion from the global financial crisis of 2008, and they see us as having a frozen political system that is unable to address our problems effectively. And, frankly, that perception is out there widely in the world. And I think it is wrong, because I think it leads to a misestimation of the latent capabilities of this country. But, frankly, we are feeding those misperceptions by not addressing our domestic problems more effectively, in my judgment. I mean, this is what I bring back when I travel abroad.

And there is a second point that I will make, in terms of whether we are a declining country or not. I was in the Foreign Service and in the government a long time. During the first 30 years of my government career, every time I returned to the United States, it was better. We had an interstate highway system. We switched to jet aircraft. Things worked better. And, for the last 20 years, every time I return to the United States, I am ashamed to see that our infrastructure works less well, is less modern than you see in other countries. If you have been to China and ridden on their high-speed rail system, it makes you ashamed to take an Amtrak train to New York. You can barely stand up on it. And in China, the trains go at twice the speed and are smooth as silk.

So, this disturbs me, as an American, because—I hate walking up escalators that do not work. [Laughter.]

And in Washington, that is an everyday experience. And we are talking about technology that was developed at the end of the 19th century, and somehow we cannot even keep our escalators working. Dammit, I wish that Congress would——

[Laughter.]

Ambassador ROY. [continuing]. Address these types of issues.

Senator RUBIO. We have a bill on escalators this week, do we not? [Laughter.]

The CHAIRMAN. Well, I am glad, Ambassador, we have given you a forum to express those——

[Laughter]

The CHAIRMAN. As one of the members here trying to get a highway mass transit bill done——

[Laughter.]

The CHAIRMAN [continuing]. We are all in favor of that.

Let me thank you both. I do have two quick questions. I want to take advantage of your expertise, here. And I leave this open to either—the first one, open to either one of you, and then the second one is for Dr. Friedberg.

The way I see it—I also sit on the Senate Finance Committee, and the way I see it, China adopting a market-determined exchange rate would not only help rebalance their economy domestically, but certainly would go a long way toward correcting some of the imbalances that exist in our bilateral trade relationship. How quickly do you think that China will move toward a market-determined exchange rate? And what, if anything, can we do to encourage or support that within China? Any of you have—either one of you have any views on that?

Ambassador ROY. It is going to take time. I think it may happen faster than we think. China is not comfortable holding trillions of dollars of foreign exchange reserves, much of which is in dollar-denominated treasury instruments. And therefore, it is actively seeking to increase trade that is settled in renminbi. And it is reaching agreements with bilateral trading partners to settle the accounts using China's currency.

But, China still does not have open capital accounts. And until it moves to open capital accounts, it cannot become a reserve currency for other countries, effectively. So, they are not there yet, and they are not ready for that step yet, but they are definitely setting that as a goal. And I think we would be blinding ourselves if we think that we can simply assume the dollar will remain the principal international trading currency, given the current trends we see in patterns of international trade.

They have already made quite rapid progress, in terms of the percentages in which their trade accounts are settled in nondollar currencies. So, it is something, I think, that we need to pay very close attention to.

We are financing ourselves 50 percent through foreign borrowing. You know, in World War II, we financed it entirely by domestic savings. But, now we are financing it by foreign borrowing. If we ever reach the point where we have to borrow in foreign currencies, then we lose control over the terms of repayment. And that is what bankrupted Asia during the Asian financial crisis. Because the short-term dollar rates were lower than borrowing in local currencies, and because the currencies seemed stable, they were borrowing in short-term dollar terms, and all of a sudden the financial crisis caused the exchange rates to go gaga, and all of a sudden, Indonesia was bankrupt overnight because of that. We do not want to move in that direction, and that is one reason why we need to get our financial system functioning well.

The CHAIRMAN. Let me turn to Dr. Friedberg.

So, with reference to our rebalancing to Asia and your comments about, while you think it is right, you think it lacks the robustness that is necessary, you mentioned the capacity—helping the capacity of our allies to be a deterrent toward the type of actions that we might be concerned with by China. If you were to say—if you were sitting in the administration and you would say, ''Here are the three, four top things that I think we should do,'' what would they be? I did not particularly care for rebalancing or pivoting, because I do not think we have ever left. The only question is, What is the degree of our engagement?

Dr. FRIEDBERG. Well, the first one is very easy to say, but, I realize, very, very difficult to accomplish. I think we are going to have to increase defense spending, in the long run, and, in particular, we are going to have to increase the resources that are devoted to the kinds of capabilities we need to counter this emerging Chinese antiaccess area denial network. I do not think that is going to happen anytime soon. I think we are trying to make do with what we have. But, I think, in the long run, that is not going to be adequate.

Related to that, I think we are going to have to develop and articulate a coherent and credible strategy for enabling ourselves to project power into the region under any circumstances in order to maintain our security commitments. One thing about the so-called rebalance or pivot, or whatever one wants to call it, that I think was not particularly well handled, was the premature discussion of the so-called air-sea battle concept, which attempts to begin to answer this question, but was not ready for prime time and has caused a lot of problems and confusion. Nevertheless, I think there is a gap there that needs to be filled. We have to have a credible story that we can tell ourselves about how we would use our forces if we needed to do so, and also to tell our allies. And we do not, at the moment.

I think, as far as assisting our friends and allies, there are a number of things—and again, some of these things are currently being done, and perhaps they could be done more—the kinds of military exercises that we have engaged in, we are about to engage in with the Philippines, also with Japan, which demonstrate to any observers that we are prepared to use force, if necessary, to help our allies defend themselves in contingencies that might involve intrusion in their territorial waters, and so on, I think send a powerful deterrent signal. There are kinds of capabilities that our friends and allies would like to buy, some of which we sell, some of which other countries, like Japan, may be willing to sell, which increase their situational awareness, enable them to better patrol and control their territorial waters and airspace. I think those things make sense.

We ought to be encouraging, even where we are not directly involved, the kinds of connections that are growing up among countries in the region that are intended to enhance their defense capabilities. Japan and Australia are talking about co-developing a new submarine for Australia. That makes sense, I think. Japan and India are engaged in naval conversations and maneuvers. Those things make sense. Even when we are not directly involved, we should be encouraging others to do things to help to maintain a balance.

The CHAIRMAN. Well, thank you both for your very valuable insights. This obviously will be a continuing source of the committee's attention. We look forward to engaging you along the way as we have different issues to pursue.

This hearing's record will remain open until the close of business tomorrow.

And, with the thanks of the committee, this hearing is adjourned.

[Whereupon, at 4:20 p.m., the hearing was adjourned.]